Legends of the Middle Ages: The Life and Legacy of Saladin

By Charles River Editors

Statue of Saladin in Damascus, Syria

About Charles River Editors

Charles River Editors was founded by Harvard and MIT alumni to provide superior editing and original writing services, with the expertise to create digital content for publishers across a vast range of subject matter. In addition to providing original digital content for third party publishers, Charles River Editors republishes civilization's greatest literary works, bringing them to a new generation via ebooks.

Visit charlesrivereditors.com for more information.

Introduction

Sculpture of Saladin in Cairo, Egypt

Saladin (1137/8-1193)

"It is equally true that his generosity, his piety, devoid of fanaticism, that flower of liberality and courtesy which had been the model of our old chroniclers, won him no less popularity in Frankish Syria than in the lands of Islam." - René Grousset

A lot of ink has been spilled covering the lives of history's most influential figures, but how much of the forest is lost for the trees? In Charles River Editors' Legends of the Middle Ages series, readers can get caught up to speed on the lives of important medieval men and women in the time it takes to finish a commute, while learning interesting facts long forgotten or never known.

During a trip to Damascus, Syria in 1958, Egyptian President Gamal Abdel Nasser visited the tomb of Saladin. It was a symbolic visit for the pan-Arab leader, who sought to unite the Arab world and restore it to its past glory. For nationalists like Nasser and devout Muslims across the Middle East, Saladin's life and reign represent the pinnacle of that glory, more than 8 centuries after his death.

Saladin is widely considered one of the greatest generals in history and one of the most famous leaders of the Middle Ages, but he remains a paradox, both in personal and in historical terms. A military genius, he first served other generals and was overshadowed, late in life, by his greatest rival, Richard I of England. He was far more admired by his Christian enemies, who extolled his chivalry, than some of his Muslim rivals, who fought him for control of Egypt and Syria in the 12th century. His Christian enemies continued his name long after it was forgotten in the Middle East, only to spark a revival of his reputation in Arab culture in the 20th century.

Revered as the flower of Arab culture, he was really a Kurd who nearly destroyed it. Taught to Egyptian children as a native born Egyptian hero, he was, in fact, Egypt's conqueror, the man who destroyed its native dynasty and suppressed the local Shi'ite sect. Praised for his mild temper and mercy, he made it his mission in the last decade of his life to destroy the Frankish states created by the First Crusade in 1099. The most powerful man in the Levant for the last ten years of his life, he died a virtual pauper after giving away his personal fortune to the poor. Having united almost all of the Levant under one rule, he left it as divided as before. He founded a dynasty that was eventually destroyed by slaves.

Nevertheless, Saladin remains both a poignant and important symbol in the Middle East over 800 years after his death, making him as relevant as ever today. *Legends of the Middle Ages: The Life and Legacy of Saladin* chronicles the historic life and reign of the famous leader, and it analyzes his influential and enduring legacy. Along with pictures of important people, places, and events, you will learn about Saladin like you never have before, in no time at all.

Saladin depicted on a 12th century coin

Chapter 1: Saladin's Early Years and Surroundings

Like all great conquerors, Saladin did not exist in a vacuum, historical or otherwise. The world he came into was greatly affected by major historical events (especially the First and Second Crusades) and his two predecessors – Zengi (c.1085-1146) and his son Nur ad-Din (1118-1174). Saladin was born in Tikrit (now in modern Iraq) circa 1138, but he spent his formative years in Damascus in Syria. Little is known about his childhood or young adult life before he joined his uncle, Shirkuh (d.1169), in his expeditions against Egypt around the age of 25 in 1163. Saladin was well-educated in ancient studies and the Qu'ran, according to the North African writer, al-Wahrani, and was fond of the city of Damascus, coming to view it as his home city rather than Tikrit.

Saladin would be a giant on the world's stage during his time, but that was not the only reason he is so well known and remembered today. His true name was not "Saladin," the westernization of his *laqab* or title, "Salah-ed-Din," ("Righteousness of the Faithful"), but the more simple "Yusuf son of Ayyub." Both hated and admired, he is one of the best-documented rulers of the Middle Ages, with two biographers who were his personal secretaries, the Kurdish historian Baha ad-Din ibn Shaddad (1145-1234) and the Persian scholar Imad-ad-Din al-Isfahani (1125-1201). Letters that he sent and received from Egypt, and later in Syria, also survive. He is frequently mentioned in in chronicles like those of Kurdish historian Ali ibn Al-Athir (1160-1233), who served for a time with Saladin's army in Syria, and William, Archbishop of Tyre (1130-1186), a Frankish crusader historian.

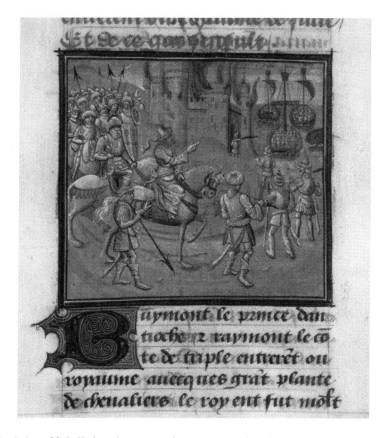

Depiction of Saladin burning a town, from a manuscript of the French translation of William of Tyre's *Historia*

According to legend, his father, a Kurdish mercenary named Najm ad-Din Ayyub (d.1173), was forced into exile the night of Saladin's birth. Ayyub had gone against his own lord to give refuge to Zengi and his troops in 1132 after the murder of a rival Christian by his brother Shirkuh, a favor Zengi repaid six years later by giving Saladin's family asylum after Ayyub (who later lent his name to his son's dynasty) was exiled.

Ayyub fell out of favor in 1146 with Zengi's son, Nur ad-Din, when he surrendered the castle of Baalbeck while being attacked, but he was able to get back into Nur ad-Din's good graces by negotiating the surrender of Damascus to Nur ad-Din in 1154. Saladin therefore began his military career serving Zengi and Nur ad-Din under his father and his uncle Shirkuh. Therefore, while his fortunes came from the Zengids, his loyalties remained within his own family.

The Zengids and Ayyubids were very much a product of their period and of the wave of Turkish invaders from the previous century. The Seljuq Turks had arrived in the early 11th century from Central Asia by way of Persia and quickly conquered most of the area of Anatolia, the Levant and North Africa, leaving only a small area around Constantinople to the Byzantine Empire (which had previously held Jerusalem and the Levant until the early seventh century). But the Seljuqs were not a cohesive group, and they quickly fell apart into a loosely organized empire of squabbling nobles.

When the Byzantine Emperor subsequently sent envoys to the Pope in Rome asking for aid against the Seljuqs, it is most likely that he asked for and expected mercenaries. Pope Urban II, for his own reasons, decided the Byzantines needed a new thing – a crusade - instead. In one of the most famous events in the Catholic Church's history, Urban II exhorted the faithful to take up arms for the Holy Land and promised them remission of their sins if they died in battle. In November 1095, according to Fulcher of Chartres, the pope said, "I, or rather the Lord, beseech you as Christ's heralds to publish this everywhere and to pers-e all people of whatever rank, foot-soldiers and knights, poor and rich, to carry aid promptly to those Christians and to destroy that vile race from the lands of our friends. I say this to those who are present, it is meant also for those who are absent. Moreover, Christ commands it." Fulcher of Chartres has Urban II continue:

> "All who die by the way, whether by land or by sea, or in battle against the pagans, shall have immediate remission of sins. This I grant them through the power of God with which I am invested. O what a disgrace if such a despised and base race, which worships demons, should conquer a people which has the faith of omnipotent God and is made glorious with the name of Christ! With what reproaches will the Lord overwhelm us if you do not aid those who, with us, profess the Christian religion! Let those who have been accustomed unjustly to wage private warfare against the faithful now go against the infidels and end with victory this war which should have been begun long ago. Let those who for a long time, have been robbers, now become knights. Let those who have been fighting against their brothers and relatives now fight in a proper way against the barbarians. Let those who have been serving as mercenaries for small pay now obtain the eternal reward. Let those who have been wearing themselves out in both body and soul now work for a double honor. Behold! on this side will be the sorrowful and poor, on that, the rich; on this side, the enemies of the Lord, on that, his friends. Let those who go not put off the journey, but rent their lands and collect money for their expenses; and as soon as winter is over and spring comes, let them eagerly set out on the way with God as their guide."

Tens of thousands of dutiful Christians thus took up arms for what would become the first of many crusades.

A disorganized European peasant army was easily destroyed by the Turks in 1096, but the army of nobles who followed later were better supplied and better trained. They took advantage of the unique circumstances of the Seljuqs' failing empire and the power vacuum left in its wake after the Seljuqs had replaced local Arab elites and traveled down through Anatolia. They took Jerusalem and large sections of the coastal Levant in 1099, two weeks before Urban II died in July of that year.

Urban II

The Crusaders' descendants proceeded to fight a losing battle to keep the Holy Land for the next two centuries. At first, they were fairly successful due to the continuing power vacuum in the Muslim Near East. However, in the first decades of the 12th century, Imad ad-Din Zengi (no relation to Saladin's biographer) came to power and became determined to retake the Levant from the European invaders.

Zengi was born in 1085, and his early life was even more inauspicious than Saladin's, marked as it was by his father's execution as a traitor to his lord, Malik-Shah, who was nominal sultan of all the Seljuqs, when Zengi was 11. Zengi grew up in Mosul, a city on the Tigris River in what is now northern Iraq, and eventually became *atabeg* there in 1127. The following year, the *atabeg* of Damascus died, sparking a power struggle between Muslim and Christian leaders for the city. An *atabeg* was a Turkish governor (in this case, one ruling for the Sultan of Damascus in the Seljuq system). Zengi became ultimately independent, the Seljuq sultanate having fallen apart following the deaths of Malik-Shah and his highly competent vizier, Nizam al-Mulk, in 1092.

Perhaps inspired by his father, who had been the practical ruler of Syria before his execution,

Zengi set out to expand his base from Mosul to Aleppo (which his father had ruled), Homs and the former Christian county of Edessa. The chronicler Ibn 'al-Adim quotes Zengi referring to himself as a "tyrant" and discusses the strong discipline that he maintained through fear over his troops. Zengi practiced a highly effective blend of ruthlessness, alliance and treachery, which did not make him unique among his rivals so much as he was simply better at it than others. He had become both hated and admired by the time of his assassination at the hands of a Frankish slave in 1146.

One problem with the Seljuq rulers, and one reason why their empire fell apart so quickly, was that they parceled out territories to their sons, so each ruler's fiefdom easily fell apart upon the death of a ruler. This was true of Zengi, as well. He left his Syrian territories to his second son, Nur ad-Din, and his Iraq territories to his first-born son. The latter dynasty survived until the 13th century.

Nur ad-Din was more of a military leader than a game player in his father's mold. William of Tyre called Nur ad-Din a great enemy of Christian Palestine but also acknowledged him as a just and courteous enemy who became deeply religious after a major illness changed his outlook on life. Shortly after his father's death, Nur ad-Din made a change in his father's long-term strategy. He decided to conquer Egypt.

There were two reasons for this. One was that he and his older brother divided up their father's realm between them, so that the brother had Zengi's Iraq possessions and Nur ad-Din held Syria. This required that he make any future expansions to the south to avoid conflict with his brother, with whom he was on cordial terms. Second, the Crusaders had come to their own conclusions in the wake of the failure of the siege of Damascus during the Second Crusade and the final loss of the County of Edessa in the north. It became clear to them that they had little hope of making any progress in Syria. Therefore, they, too, needed to look south. Thus, both the Crusaders and Nur ad-Din now looked toward Egypt.

Egypt was a tempting prize, albeit not an easy one. The problem for the Crusaders was that they had a powerful Syria on their flank every time they tried to invade Egypt. The problem for Nur ad-Din, over and above any issue of religious conflict, was that uniting Egypt and Syria was almost impossible with the Crusader States lying in the way.

The Crusaders made their move first in the 1150s. The last Egyptian caliph, Al-Adid (1149-71), came to the throne in 1154, though the real power lay with his astute vizier, Shawar (d.1169). Shawar was in favor of allying with the Crusaders, which was not an especially popular position, and he had accrued a large fortune at the expense of the people, which was also not popular. However, he was good at manipulating the local emirs, who were characterized by crusader sources as weak and easily swayed. He also needed to do something to protect Egypt from her many enemies.

Allying with the Franks was not as odd a pairing as it might have seemed. In border regions between Islam and Christianity, like the Middle East and the Iberian Peninsula, during times when a victor was not clear and the battle went back and forth, even intense religious differences gave way to more regional and even clan or personal, differences. The gulf between the Shi'ite Fatimids, who had established their dynasty in the ninth century, and the Sunni Turkish Syrians, who had come almost as late to the scene as the Franks and were culturally almost as alien, was huge. Since the Franks had recently taken Egypt's last stronghold, Ascalon, this made them Egypt's *de facto* neighbors. It is unclear how much Shawar was aware of the ultimate goal of joining Syria with Egypt in the eyes of Syrian warlords like Nur ad-Din, but he was certainly aware that the Egyptian dynasty was as much at risk of being as completely destroyed by a Syrian Muslim invasion as by a Christian one. He therefore made the unpopular alliance with the relatively weaker and more over-stretched power.

The Syrians, for their part, were rough, violent, well-versed in war, and centered in their family loyalties. After Nur ad-Din sent his lieutenant Shirkuh (Saladin's uncle) to invade the country and break the Crusader hold, Shawar responded by expelling Shirkuh and accepting the Crusaders back, even brokering a treaty between the Franks and the young Caliph. It was not until 1169 that Shirkuh was able to invade and hold Egypt successfully, consolidating his power by executing Shawar. Shirkuh, however, did not live long to enjoy his success, for he died two months later.

Chapter 2: The Conquest of Egypt

19th-century depiction of the victorious Saladin, by Gustave Doré.

It is at this point, at the age of 31, that Saladin was finally able to shine. Though Zengi's intervention in his family fortunes had greatly affected his life, he was still just an eight year old child when Zengi was assassinated. Therefore, his main lord had always been Nur ad-Din and his main influence had been his father and his uncle, Shirkuh, both of whom served Zengi and then Nur ad-Din.

Saladin had fought with his uncle on Shirkuh's Egyptian expeditions since 1164. The Ayyubids were clannish and close-knit, so Saladin's position in his uncle's army was literal nepotism, but this familial opportunism did not detract from his ability. M.C. Lyons and D.E.P Jackson, in their definitive biography, *Saladin: The Politics of the Holy War* (1982), note that Shirkuh picked Saladin as his *aide-de-camp* over his own sons, an indication of Shirkuh's recognition of his nephew's innate abilities. Shirkuh had a reputation (reported even by his enemies, like William of Tyre) for winning the loyalty of his men by living among them and sharing their hardships. Shirkuh was a coarse, short, fat man whose fierce temper that had gotten his family exiled from Tikrit, but he was also a shrewd general and a beloved military leader.

It is probably no coincidence that Saladin, too, acquired a reputation for living with his men and rousing their undying loyalty, though his appearance and personal habits were more moderate, like his nominal lord Nur ad-Din. No account of his life definitively explains what Saladin learned from Shirkuh, but a comparison of what contemporaries thought were their respective military strengths demonstrates that Saladin's experience, shrewdness, strategy, specific skills in exciting loyalty in his troops, work ethic, and even expeditious ruthlessness did not grow in a vacuum. He probably picked much of it up from observing his uncle over the six years he served him in Egypt.

For example, in one major battle with the Franks near Giza, Saladin was given charge of the right flank. He chose to put the baggage with his uncle in the middle (contemporary Muslim sources put Saladin in the middle), giving the impression of a weak center. Allowing a soft center so that the enemy can attack it and be surrounded by a pincer movement is an old tactic and very effective with a disciplined army that will hold together while being divided. Hannibal had famously used it to destroy a Roman army at the decisive Battle of Cannae over a thousand years earlier, and generals have been trying to use it with the same success ever since. In his own battle, Saladin successfully executed his part of the pincer and helped ensure the Franks were routed. This kind of experience would serve him well when his uncle was gone.

Shirkuh had ordered the assassination of Shawar, leaving a power vacuum upon his death. The young Caliph and his advisors chose Saladin as the new governor, according to Ibn al-Athir, because Saladin was perceived to be the weakest candidate and the least likely to be able to rally the Syrian emirs. Al-Wahrani claims that Saladin was chosen out of respect for his family's prowess, while Imad ad-Din claims that the Syrian faction forced Saladin on the Caliph. Whatever the reasons, Saladin did not simply walk into his position. He was forced to earn the loyalty of the emirs and make the Caliph's faction bend to his will, though he did so in part by making small concessions and using security matters (such as the Frankish invasion) to put down revolts and execute any emirs that opposed him.

There were many such revolts, perhaps exacerbated by the Syrians' practice of confiscating the Egyptian emirs' goods at will. According to Syrian chronicler Ibn Abi Tayy, "When a Turk saw an Egyptian, he took his clothes." Ibn Abi Tayy even accused the Syrians of evicting Egyptians from their houses without cause. Soon, there were riots in Cairo, the power center of the

Caliphate. According to Abu Salih, Maqrizi and a letter by Saladin to Baghdad, Saladin was, as late as the summer of 1172, losing money to European merchants while facing sporadic-but-rising insurrection in a country in debt. Turning the situation around took far more than the nepotism that had put him at his uncle's side in the first place, and his success bode well and was a sign of his future greatness.

One of the first things Saladin did, aside from playing the Egyptian emirs against each other, was to consolidate his position by employing nepotism himself. He made the judicious appointment of trusted relatives to several important posts in his army and even got Nur ad-Din to send his father to Egypt. Unlike his later image as a patriot of Egypt (which was frequently invoked for propaganda purposes by the pan-Arab Nasser regime in the mid-20th century), Saladin did not choose to keep the old elite of Egyptian emirs, let alone the Caliphate, in place. Retaining the Caliphate would have been an option if he had chosen to remain a vassal to Nur ad-Din, but he was already moving away from that allegiance. Instead, he set out to destroy the old Egyptian Fatimid leadership and replace it completely with Syrians, encouraging his own men to have children and fathering four of his own by 1173. He did not father any children until he had passed the age of 30.

It is unknown at what point Saladin decided to defy Nur ad-Din, though he clearly engaged in a policy of expansion of power to balance out the problems going on in Egypt almost from the moment of Shirkuh's death. But it is entirely possible that he had no long-term plan at the time and only later became clear to him that expansion, especially east back into the Levant, would bring him into eventual and inevitable conflict with Nur ad-Din. Similarly, Nur ad-Din's motives for growing tired of waiting for Saladin are not entirely clear – or, at least, their origins are not clear. Some historians claimed that Nur ad-Din felt that Saladin was not sending him enough tribute from Egypt for the jihad back in Syria, but Imad ad-Din insists that Nur ad-Din did not want the money that Saladin later offered him.

Up to this point, Saladin had been no more a religious man than his uncle or Zengi, even according to his own biographers. However, the conquest of Egypt changed his outlook. Egypt was rich, fertile and chaotic enough to present him with many of the challenges that eventually made him a great general, yet also weak enough to provide him with an achievable conquest to retain. As part of this new awareness of his increased status in the world, he gave up wine and began to take the rules of Islam more seriously. This was a good thing, for he needed a clear head to deal with an assassination attempt later that year by the Egyptian faction. He then defeated a Crusader army near Damietta, before attacking Darum the following year.

In Egypt, Saladin was perhaps already trying to establish his legitimacy as a devout and just Muslim ruler who was replacing an older, corrupt elite that had fallen away from the true faith. Despite Saladin's later reputation for culture and gentility, fostered by his two biographers, even the faithful Imad ad-Din complained about his master's retainers, whom he referred to as "rough companions." Saladin therefore needed to create a basis for his right to rule that successfully counteracted both the hereditary legitimacy of those he overthrew and the rough lack of Arab culture in his own family. The intense loyalties within his own clan could only take him so far as long as they remained known solely as mercenaries and military governors.

Saladin now began to consolidate his power in Egypt, which included suppressing the local Shi'ite worship via the establishment of Sunni madrasas, pushing aside the minor Caliph (who conveniently died in 1171 and was replaced by a Sunni Abbassid Caliph after the Shi'ite emirs were massacred), and raising himself up as a virtual equal to his erstwhile lord, Nur ad-Din. All of these things were perfectly standard for an ambitious Seljuq leader and were signs that an astute leader like Nur ad-Din could not possibly miss.

Saladin soon made his intentions even clearer, first by ignoring several letters from Nur ad-Din, failing to support Nur ad-Din in wars to the north with his nephews after his older brother's death in 1170, and in attacks on Jerusalem in 1171 and 1173. His lack of support effectively announced his intention to declare independence from Nur ad-Din, and he may have been relying on the Crusader States as a buffer for protection. Recognizing the trend and worrying that the rich breadbasket of Egypt was slipping from his grasp, Nur ad-Din reluctantly decided to wage a war against Saladin before Saladin could become too powerful.

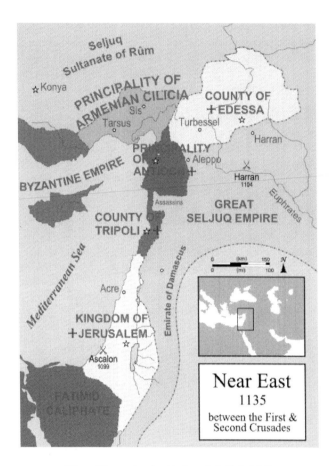

Map of the region just before Saladin's birth

However, he died on the eve of the invasion in 1174, from a similar illness to that suffered by Shirkuh. Several of Saladin's rivals or obstacles died at opportune times for Saladin, suggesting to some enemies that someone – perhaps the Assassins if not Saladin, himself – had poisoned them. Nur ad-Din left behind a minor son, As-Salih Ismail al-Malik (1163-81). Saladin immediately declared his regency over As-Salih, married Nur ad-Din's widow, and effectively replaced his former lord. Al-Malik conveniently died in 1181 at the age of 18, not having reached his majority or taken power.

Chapter 3: Civil War in Syria

This transfer of power to the new dynasty did not occur immediately. Any plans Saladin had of uniting the realms were put on hold as he engaged in a civil war with other claimants to Nur ad-Din's throne. His main difficulty arose from the fact that he had no legitimate basis for ruling in Syria, or for deposing the rightful Caliph and ruling Egypt for that matter. He was not related to Nur ad-Din, who had a living son and living adult brothers, as did Nur ad-Din's nominal lord in Baghdad. Saladin was only one of Nur ad-Din's mercenaries, and he had earned the distrust of Nur ad-Din and the Syrians concerning his devotion (or lack of it) to jihad by failing to provide financial assistance to Syria during the warring with the Christians. As such, Saladin had to pursue his goals in Syria through subterfuge and warfare.

Saladin's first break came in 1174, when the emir of Damascus reluctantly asked for his aid after being attacked by another former captain of Nur ad-Din, Gumushtigin of Aleppo. Gumushtigin had seized Nur ad-Din's heir, As-Salih, and tried to seize all of Nur ad-Din's territory. Saladin crossed the desert from Egypt with a select cavalry of 700. When he arrived in Damascus, he was welcomed as a liberator and immediately took over the castle there.

After leaving his brother to administer Damascus and taking the town of Hamah, Saladin then besieged Gumushtigin in Aleppo. Fearing Saladin's intentions, As-Salih himself begged the populace not to give in. The siege, as well as one made against the well-defended fortress at Homs, was thwarted by an attack by 13 Assassins, requested by Gumushtigin, and an opportunistic attack by the crusader Raymond III, Count of Tripoli (1140-87), who was at times both Saladin's enemy and ally. The Count of Tripoli was greatly respected in Europe, and William of Tyre described him glowingly:

"A man of slender build, extremely spare, of medium height and swarthy complexion. His hair was straight and rather dark in color. He had piercing eyes and carried his shoulders very erect. He was prompt and vigorous in action, gifted with equanimity and foresight, and temperate in his use of both food and drink, far more than the average man. He showed munificence towards strangers, but towards his own people he was not so lavish. He was fairly well-lettered, an accomplishment which he had acquired while a prisoner among the enemy, at the expense of much effort, aided greatly, however, by his natural keenness of mind. Like King [Amalric I], he eagerly sought the knowledge contained in written works. He was indefatigable in asking questions if there happened to be anyone present who in his opinion was capable of answering."

The siege had harmed Saladin's reputation in Syria because he had laid siege to a city where his former lord's son was taking refuge. This provided a propaganda boon for his Muslim enemies, but Saladin quickly raised the siege and used the crusader attack to show that he was defending the faith from the Franks. His fortunes in Syria began to change again when he was finally able to take Homs in March 1175.

His next rival was Saif ad-Din (d.1180), a nephew of Nur ad-Din, who marched against him in Hama with a superior army the following month. Worried, Saladin first tried to sue for terms, but was unable to win them. By judiciously deploying his forces on the high ground, he was able to use his battle-hardened soldiers (who had gained experienced from the civil war in Egypt) to crush the other army's superior numbers. This would not be the last time Saladin used this tactic, or that it would be successful. From this point onward, Saladin declared himself the ruler of Syria and eased as-Salih out. In Cairo, gold coins were minted with his new title: al-Malik an-Nasir Yusuf Ayyub, ala ghaya ("the King Strong to Aid, Joseph son of Job; exalted be the standard").

The Cairo Citadel, ordered constructed by Saladin in the 1170s.

Saif ad-Din and Gumushtigin were not truly crushed, however, until 1176. Saladin defeated Saif ad-Din in battle in the spring and then made a truce with Gumushtigin and As-Salih in June, only slightly deterred by a solar eclipse he considered an omen and a nearly successful assassination attempt. During intense hand-to-hand fighting that drove Saladin's left flank back, Saladin personally led a charge that helped rout the Zengids, leaving Saladin in possession of the enemy's supplies. In a cunning move designed to build loyalty, he freed the Zengid prisoners of war and spread the loot around his army without taking anything of value himself.

Saladin spent the rest of the summer punishing the Assassins for the assassination attempt by laying waste to their territory. This had little effect, and he ultimately broke a truce with the Crusaders to ally with the Assassins instead. It was this alliance, and a battle at Tell Jezer in November, that perhaps explains Saladin's later hatred of the military orders, especially the Assassins' traditional enemies, the Knights Templar. He lost the battle because the Templars were able to reach his bodyguard and cut them down. Saladin escaped, but he had learned a lesson about these Frankish enemies who were every bit as hardened and disciplined as his men. He engaged in skirmishes with the Crusaders in 1178 and then took a major Templar castle, Jacob's Ford, at the end of August in 1179. In 1180, a drought forced him to agree to a peace with Baldwin IV, the last King of Jerusalem (1161-85).

Medieval depiction of Baldwin IV's coronation

Saladin spent the summer entangled in a potentially damaging dispute between an ally, Nur al-Din (to whom he had given refuge), and Nur al-Din's father in law, the powerful Seljuq Sultan of Rum who accused Nur al-Din of abusing his daughter and demanded back her dowry. 1181 was wasted on fruitless attempts to consolidate the conquest of Yemen, but it did bring one bright spot with the death of one of Saladin's great rivals – Saif al-Din – in June.

Saladin did not marry Nur ad-Din's widow, Ismat ad-Din Khatun (d.1186), until 1176, when he defeated his Zengid rivals and became *de facto* ruler of Syria. In spite of the generally restricted status of women in medieval Islamic society, she was no shrinking violet and was the actual hereditary heir to Damascus. Despite the cold, political nature of their alliance, and his having other wives, Saladin was greatly devoted to her until her death ten years later. According to William of Tyre, she rebuffed a siege by King Amalric I of Jerusalem (1136-74) in the wake of her first husband's death, forcing him to accept her terms after a siege of two weeks.

Chapter 4: The Road to Hattin

By 1180, Saladin had consolidated his power in both Egypt and Syria, but he still could not join his two realms because of the obstacle that had once protected his Egyptian realm as a buffer zone: the Crusader States. He now decided to root out the Christian principalities from the Levant, even the Byzantines, though this was not a new goal. He had begun harrying the Crusaders and pushing them back out of Egypt even before he had finished establishing his power there. However, he had also allied with them against other Muslim rivals from time to time. With his triumph over his Muslim rivals complete, he now turned on his erstwhile Christian foes. Attacks on Muslim caravans and other violations of truces by notorious crusader, Raynald of Chatillon (c.1125-1187), beginning in 1181, gave Saladin the pretext for this change in tack.

Depiction of Raynald of Châtillon torturing Patriarch Aimery of Antioch, from the manuscript of William of Tyre's *Historia*)

How much of this new call to jihad in the 12th century was genuine religious fervor for Saladin and his predecessors, and how much was cynical political aggrandizement, remains subject to debate. Zengi, in particular, was ruthless in his pursuit of power, engaging in assassinations and betrayals of other Muslim leaders far more than engaging directly with crusaders. Nur ad-Din and Saladin both continued this pattern of accruing power. Zengi was also not portrayed as a good Muslim by some contemporaries, nor was was Shirkuh. In his hostile account of Zengi's assassination, Damascene chronicler Ibn al-Qalanisi claims that Zengi was killed while drunk, a major violation of Islamic religious code, implying that this was a common occurrence.

On the other hand, Zengi showed considerable zeal in attacking the Crusaders once he began to engage with the Crusader States and does at least appear to have seen them as major rivals for Damascus and the rest of Syria. Also, while contemporary accounts are mixed on how devout Saladin was (he never, for example, went on *hajj* – pilgrimage – to Mecca), he was reported as abstaining from alcohol and other excesses following his conquest of Egypt, and he engaged the

Crusaders far more than previous or contemporary *atabegs*.

Thus, it's probably fair to say there was a bit of both the worldly and the divine in his motivations and methods. Saladin, despite carefully cultivating the image of a holy warrior through his biographers, was no different in this respect from either his Muslim or his Christian enemies, as the Crusaders had similarly mixed motives and methods. He certainly believed, but perhaps not quite as devoutly as he claimed. Nevertheless, it was necessary to promote himself as a jihadist Sultan favored by God in order to rally other Muslims to his cause, and it was made all the more important by the fact that Saladin, like the other *atabegs*, represented a usurping class from West Asia that the old Arab elite resented and did not respect. Also, Saladin had deposed the Egyptian caliph and usurped the rightful successor of his own lord. Caliphs, as descendants of the Prophet Muhammad, were considered to be major religious leaders, even when they had been reduced to weak puppets in secular power. Thus, it was necessary for Saladin to establish himself as the legitimate leader of Syria and Egypt by playing the righteous sultan guided by God in holy war via jihad. This required the language of holy war, even when Saladin warred with other Muslims.

The Crusaders had an advantage in this kind of war, despite being decentralized in secular power and relatively weak militarily compared to their Muslim neighbors. Christian religious authority was strongly centralized in two ancient poles – the Papacy in Rome and the Patriarchate in Constantinople. Christians were also quite strict in which authority they accepted. Latins might work with the Byzantines, and the Pope might choose to correspond with the Patriarch as a fellow vicar in Christ, but this alliance was always tenuous. Latins did not recognize the authority of the Patriarch, and the Byzantines had the same view toward the Pope. This allowed secular leaders to align themselves according to clear religious authorities, and to use their endorsement to accrue support for crusades, something non-caliphate rulers struggled to do in promoting Islamic jihad. Christian religious authority, older and better organized, also had longevity that Muslim religious authority lacked. Perhaps most importantly, the Christians weren't warring with each other, whereas the division between the two main Muslim sects, majority Sunnism and minority Shi'ism, played a huge factor in the conquest of Egypt and left the two sides downright hostile towards each other. In comparison, the division between Latin and Greek Christianity was only a century old at that point.

Another trend was occurring that ultimately doomed Christian Palestine, while introducing a great long-term threat to the Islamic World of which leaders in the east like Saladin were, at best, only vaguely aware. This involved what was going on in Europe. Even as the fortunes of the Crusaders in Palestine gradually declined, other crusades and other expansions against Muslims closer to home were far more successful. By the time Saladin won the Battle of Hattin, the Muslim region of Al-Andalus had long since fragmented and was in the process of a terminal reduction and decline, despite the best efforts of two major waves of powerful jihadists from

North Africa, the Almoravids and the Almohads, and by 1130, Norman mercenaries had wrested Sicily and southern Italy from the Muslims (who had taken it from the Byzantines) and established a kingdom there. It remained in Christian hands thereafter. Thus, while Saladin and other Turkish leaders were in the process of expelling the Latin Christians from the Middle East, the Latins were expelling the Muslims from Europe and blocking them from eventual access to the Americas, gradually forming the geopolitical structure that exists today.

Focused closer to home, Saladin faced a clear threat in the Crusader States that went even beyond religion. Because they held the coastline from Byzantine Anatolia down to the Persian Gulf, Christian realms lined the entire western border of Syria. They also held the entire coastline at arm's length from Syria, even blocking it from the Gulf and any land connection with Egypt. Saladin would proceed to hound the Kingdom of Jerusalem, but at the same time, they were able to harry Egypt from both land and sea. They could also mount relief crusades from Europe by these routes.

With all of Syria under his control, Saladin could now deal with this long-term threat. He was aided by luck in the fortuitous weakening of the Frankish dynasty in Jerusalem. First, Amalric I died suddenly in 1174, while in the middle of a dispute with one of the military religious orders, the Knights Templar. His son, Baldwin IV succeeded him. Though Baldwin was an able leader in many ways, he was still a minor and had also contracted leprosy as a child. This ensured that he could never father children of his own and resulted in bitter disputes over the succession even during his lifetime. The succession eventually went to his sister, Sibylla (1160-90), and her second husband, Guy de Lusignan (1150-94). His immediate successor was Sibylla's eight-year-old son by her first husband. However, Baldwin V only lived until 1186.

13th century depiction of Amalric I

Though an able leader, Baldwin was excoriated by the Andalusian traveler, Ibn Jubayr (1145-1217), as a "pig," despite the writer's reluctant admission that Muslims under Latin rule in the area did better than those under Muslim rule in Syria. Writing about his trip to Palestine in 1185, Ibn Jubayr, a great supporter of Saladin, also referred to Baldwin's mother, Agnes of Courteney, an able regent after his father's sudden death, as a "sow." Though this harsh attitude was partly due to Baldwin being Christian, and the natural animosities between the two faiths, it also stemmed from Muslim disgust at Baldwin's leprosy, which they perceived as a sign of God's displeasure. Despite loyal support from writers like William of Tyre, the strength of the King's power over his own subjects was also weakened by the Franks' own disgust at his condition, about which they had similar feelings. In spite of this, Baldwin served as ably as he could until his death in March 1185.

Medieval depiction of the traveler Ibn Jubayr, who met and wrote about Saladin.

Shortly after her son's death, Sibylla was crowned and her husband, Guy, became King Consort, since women like Sibylla were not expected to lead men into battle. Guy was an affable man but not perceived as a very good military leader. In fact, he had angered Baldwin by allowing Reynaud de Chatillon to pillage Muslim territories in violation of treaties and had been deposed as Baldwin's successor in favor of Guy's stepson, Baldwin V.

Guy was so unpopular in the Kingdom that the Frankish nobles demanded the more politically astute Sibylla divorce him before she could be crowned. She agreed to do so on the condition that she be allowed to choose her next husband herself. They agreed, not expecting her to be like Odysseus' wife Penelope in cunning. She divorced Guy and then promptly chose him all over again as her husband, crowning him as her consort. She bore him two daughters, who died along with her of fever in 1190 while they were on crusade. The title passed to her sister, continuing down the female line for the next century.

Unfortunately for the Kingdom of Jerusalem, Guy was no Odysseus. Taking poor advice from Reynaud de Chatillon and an unusually fanatical Grand Master of the Templars, Gerard de Ridefort, he engaged Saladin at a place called the Horns of Hattin, not far from Jerusalem, on July 4, 1187. Gerard, having arrived in the country in the late 1170s, was still filled with a crusader's zeal and lacked the more usual sense of regional *realpolitik* that his predecessors, Arnold de Torroja and Odo de St. Amand, had possessed. He advocated a reckless attack uphill against the Muslim forces between two ridges (the "horns") that doomed the Crusader effort.

The Horns of Hattin today

Saladin was not passive in the encounter. He had drawn out the Crusaders from their water source by besieging and taking the nearby castle of Tiberias as a feint. Then he deliberately set himself on the ridge at Hattin and had built fires on either side of the Crusader army's passage to cut them off from water. This made the Crusaders hot and thirsty, weakening them even further when Saladin's army swept down upon them. One of Saladin's biographers, Baha ad-Din ibn Shaddad, explained that the Franks "were closely beset as in a noose, while still marching on as though being driven to death that they could see before them, convinced of their doom and destruction and themselves aware that the following day they would be visiting their graves."

Medieval illustration of the battle

With their access to water and retreat line cut off, the crusaders made one last desperate attempt to break through. Ibn al-Athir wrote the following account based off the recollections of Saladin's son, al-Afdal:

"When the king of the Franks was on the hill with that band, they made a formidable charge against the Muslims facing them, so that they drove them back to my father. I looked towards him and he was overcome by grief and his complexion pale. He took hold of his beard and advanced, crying out "Give the lie to the Devil!" The Muslims rallied, returned to the fight and climbed the hill. When I saw that the Franks withdrew, pursued by the Muslims, I shouted for joy, 'We have beaten them!' But the Franks rallied and charged again like the first time and drove the Muslims back to my father. He acted as he had done on the first occasion and the Muslims turned upon the Franks and drove them back to the hill. I again shouted, 'We have beaten them!' but my father rounded on me and said, 'Be quiet! We have not beaten them until that tent [Guy's] falls.' As he was speaking to me, the tent fell. The sultan dismounted, prostrated himself in thanks to God Almighty and wept for joy."

With that, the Crusader army was destroyed. Both Gerard and Guy were captured, as well as the noble brigand, Raynald, and they were all brought to Saladin's tent. Saladin let the thirsty men drink water, but he quickly turned his attention to Raynald and accused him of violating his oaths. In response, Raynald stated, "Kings have always acted thus. I did nothing more." After that response, Saladin grabbed his sword and personally beheaded Raynald, shocking his other prisoners and no doubt leaving them thinking it would soon be their turn. He then explained, "It is not the wont of kings, to kill kings; but that man had transgressed all bounds, and therefore did I treat him thus. This man was only killed because of his maleficence and perfidy."

The remaining Templars and Hospitallers were executed on Saladin's orders. Saladin's secretary explained, "Saladin ordered that they should be beheaded, choosing to have them dead rather than in prison. With him was a whole band of scholars and sufis and a certain number of devout men and ascetics, each begged to be allowed to kill one of them, and drew his sword and rolled back his sleeve. Saladin, his face joyful, was sitting on his dais, the unbelievers showed black despair". Members of the military religious orders were not allowed to offer ransom beyond their own belts and swords, and all of them refused to apostasize. Gerard and Guy were both eventually ransomed at great cost, and Gerard died in battle on October 1.

It is estimated that only about 3,000 of the Christians survived the battle, leaving Palestine at Saladin's mercy. A number of outposts quickly fell, and Saladin then moved on to Jerusalem, which negotiated a surrender to him via a knight named Balin on October 2, 1187. Saladin had considered attacking the city and slaughtering its inhabitants, but the surrender avoided this. Even so, thousands of poor Christians who could not afford to ransom themselves were sold into slavery, but Saladin also allowed Jews back into the city for the first time in nearly a century. Saladin was at the very height of his power and seemed to have triumphed utterly. Save for one port, Tyre, all of the Crusader States had been conquered.

Chapter 5: The Third Crusade

Unfortunately for Saladin, three factors wrecked his plans, though not completely. First, the defeat at Hattin and the loss of Jerusalem galvanized the Franks in Europe in a way that previous defeats, and even the loss of Ascalon (which had precipitated the Second Crusade) had not done. Though interest had been flagging in the Crusades to that point, suddenly, with such a clear enemy, it revived and crystallized. Second, Tyre held out against Saladin's forces and provided an entry for the Crusaders to land and establish a beachhead. Ironically, Saladin had overlooked the more important strategic target of Tyre to go after Jerusalem first. Now, he could not take it.

Third, there was a leader in Europe that would prove to be Saladin's equal in mettle and desire to fight in religious war. Richard I of England (1157-1199) did not originally want to go, since he was focused on consolidating his own power base in his mother, Eleanor's, vast grand duchy in Aquitaine in southwestern France. Eleanor, a powerful and controversial figure, was later accused in 13th and 14th century histories like the *Chronique abrégé* and the *Chronique de Flanders* of having had an affair with Saladin, even though he was only 11 when she and her first husband were in Palestine during the Second Crusade. Richard was not motivated by racy stories about his mother's sojourn on crusade to go, himself.

The shock of the news about Hattin, however, was. The exhortation of some chroniclers, a mixture of shaming and flattery, cast him as the knight to defeat Saladin and revive the Crusader States. Unlike some Frankish writers in Palestine, like the now-departed William of Tyre, who had written with grudging admiration about their Muslim foes, many European chroniclers felt quite differently about Saladin. Joachim de Fiore, a Calabrian monk, prophesied that the seven heads of the dragon in the Book of Revelation were seven historical figures who had threatened or would threaten the world, with Saladin being the sixth, the last herald before the Antichrist. Richard was strongly urged to go to Palestine and engage with Saladin. Finally, in 1189, two years after the Battle of Hattin and the fall of Jerusalem, he did. Part of what allowed him to do so was the death of his father Henry that year, as well as his ability to leave his youngest brother behind in England as regent and his mother to administer Aquitaine.

17ᵗʰ century portrait of Richard the Lionheart

Richard was not the only leader to go, though he was arguably the best in military matters, and the two that went with him were also great leaders in their own right. The aged Frederick I Barbarossa, Holy Roman Emperor (1122-1190), was already a legendary knight when he set out for the Holy Land. Unfortunately, he drowned in a river accidentally on the way, dealing a great blow to the crusade before it had even began in earnest. Second was Philip Augustus of France (1165-1223), a shrewd and politically astute ruler who would end up diplomatically worming his way into possession of most of his Norman rival's possessions from Richard's brother and successor John after Richard's death. Richard and Philip were allies, even friends, but also strong personalities who distrusted each other. Also, Philip resented being in the shadow of Richard's military prowess, which was regarded more highly than Philip's diplomacy. Still, he was intelligent enough not to show it, or to keep from going on crusade with Richard. In fact, both kings had desired to go but did not want to if it would leave the other rival at home.

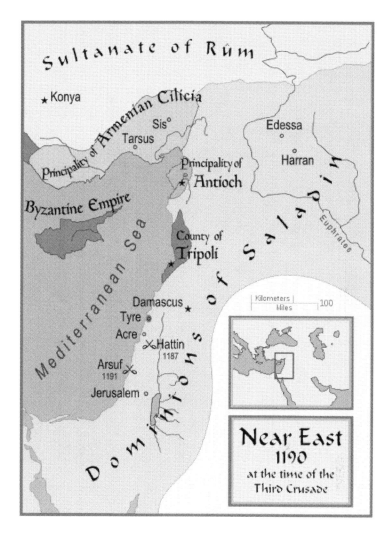

Saladin greeted the news with wariness, but he still felt confident that he could wreck the crusade, especially after Frederick Barbarossa's death. After all, English and French rulers could not stay in the Holy Land forever.

By now, however, Saladin was also running on borrowed time. Now in his 50s, he had been campaigning almost constantly for over a quarter of a century and it was taking its toll. He was old, while Richard was still young and vigorous, the same age as Saladin had been when he had subdued and conquered Egypt. Saladin was finally about to meet his match.

Richard and Philip's arrival at Acre with a large army on June 8, 1191 was greeted with joy and relief by the remaining Latin Christians living there, especially when Richard, still sick from scurvy, oversaw the siege and successful capitulation of the city.

Depiction of Philip (right) and Richard accepting the keys to Acre; from the Grandes Chroniques de France.

As the crusaders took Acre, Saladin himself employed delaying tactics, including saddling Richard with 2700 prisoners and their families near Acre. Perceiving them (probably correctly) as a major security threat that could retake the town if he left them behind, and unable to take them with or provision them, Richard engaged in the most ruthless and brutal act of his life. He massacred them all, including their families, in front of Saladin's horrified army. Saladin's soldiers attempted to break through the crusader lines to save them, but Richard's troops held them back. All told, the crusaders killed an estimated 3,000 Muslims, including women and children. Saladin biographer Baha ad-Din ibn Shaddad wrote of the slaughter, "The motives of this massacre are differently told; according to some, the captives were slain by way of reprisal for the death of those Christians whom the Musulmans had slain. Others again say that the king of England, on deciding to attempt the conquest of Ascalon, thought it unwise to leave so many prisoners in the town after his departure. God alone knows what the real reason was."

Alhough Baha ad-Din reports that Saladin retaliated by killing all Frankish prisoners between August 28 and September 10, Saladin had learned a harsh lesson about his new enemy. He had at last encountered a leader who was as ruthless, if not more so, than he was, and it sent a clear signal to Saladin that he could not expect to play on Richard's very conditional mercy. Even so, the two rulers treated each other with courtesy and respect, exchanging gifts and correspondence, though they never met in person.

Richard next moved his forces to Arsuf, where the last major battle of the Third Crusade would be fought on September 7. During the morning fighting, Richard's left flank began to waver. Richard was able to rally those men and then decided that instead of reinforcing his left, he would use his right to attack Saladin's left. According to the *Itinerarium Regis Ricardi*, a Latin prose account of the Third Crusade, "King Richard pursued the Turks with singular ferocity, fell upon them and scattered them across the ground. No one escaped when his sword made contact with them; wherever he went his brandished sword cleared a wide path on all sides. Continuing his advance with untiring sword strokes, he cut down that unspeakable race as if he were reaping the harvest with a sickle, so that the corpses of Turks he had killed covered the ground everywhere for the space of half a mile."

Depiction of Richard the Lionheart at the Battle of Arsuf, by Gustave Doré.

After routing Saladin's army at Arsuf, Richard wanted to retake Jerusalem immediately, but he was strongly advised against it. Though he had won a victory, his force was now too small and could not be replenished. Once the centerpiece of the Crusader States and the prize for which the entire First Crusade had fought, Jerusalem was now a strategic albatross that could not be properly defended or held by a visiting army. Richard very reluctantly turned away from his greatest goal.

Also thwarted in an attempt to invade Egypt, Richard eventually used his victories to negotiate with Saladin, and the correspondence they carried out became legendary for its chivalry, and it helped make and cement Saladin's legacy in the West. Having heard that Richard lost a horse at Arsuf, Saladin personally sent him two horses as a replacement. Richard even went so far as to solve the issue of Jerusalem by proposing that his sister marry Saladin's brother.

Ultimately, the leaders agreed on a three-year truce on September 2, 1192 that would leave Jerusalem in Muslim hands but allow Christian pilgrims into the city as well. With that, Richard headed back home, where he was facing the prospect of collusion between Philip and his brother back in Europe. Indeed, he was captured and held for ransom by Frankish enemies on the way home, despite returning in the company of friends, the Templars.

Chapter 6: Death and Legacy

Though defeated in battle, Saladin essentially scored a strategic victory by retaining Jerusalem during the Third Crusade, but the leader was too weary to savor the victory, and the damage Richard had done during his year in Palestine was just enough to revive the Crusader States. Saladin returned to Damascus and fell ill from a fever, which killed him on March 4, 1193. Shortly before his death, he drew up his will and gave away all of his possessions to the poor, retaining just a few piece of gold and silver for himself. This was a traditionally humble death for a pious prince, and he was buried in a simple wooden box.

As soon as Saladin was buried, his great empire began to fall apart. He left behind 17 sons and various brothers who squabbled over his realm. In the traditional Turkish way, he had divided up leadership of the various areas among his relatives, which proved disastrous as his once large empire was quickly ripped asunder by fratricidal war. The competence of his sons ranged from the foolish (Al-Afdal, who only ruled Damascus for three years before being deposed) to the destructive (Al-Aziz Uthman, who took Egypt and tried to tear down the Pyramids before dying in a hunting accident in 1198). The much-reduced Ayyubid sultanate eventually fell to a brother, Al-Adil. He continued the line until the dynasty was destroyed by a combination of revolt among its slave soldiers, the Mamluks, and invasion by the Mongols in the 1250s. Since Al-Adil and his sons had little interest in continuing Saladin's attacks on the Crusaders, it fell to the Mamluks to destroy the last of the Crusader States in 1291.

Despite his many successes, Saladin was rather quickly forgotten by his Muslim contemporaries after his death. Only 42 years after Saladin had captured the much-fought-over Jerusalem, his nephew, Al-Kamil, was willing to give it back, and the Crusaders themselves were not especially willing to take it. His empire almost immediately fell apart, and the Christians returned to and rebuilt many of their former possessions. Within six decades, his dynasty was replaced by one of former slaves, the Mamluks. Very few of his building works now survive. As with most rulers of the Middle East, Saladin's successes during his lifetime were largely ephemeral.

A century later, the Islamic Ottoman Empire replaced the Seljuq Empire, and the Ottoman Turks remained in power in the Levant and the eastern part of the Mediterranean until the 20th century. Constantinople fell to an Ottoman sultan in 1453. Blocked in the east, the Franks centralized power into various kingdoms and turned their attention back west to Europe and the New World. With no Christian enemies to fight anymore, the historical memory of the Crusades largely faded for Muslims in the Middle East, and Saladin's memory faded with it.

It's often said that the winners write the history books, but it's very rare for the winners to have such a positive view of the enemy. For Saladin, however, this was exactly the case. It would be the European Christians who kept his name and reputation alive, and they even admired him, though this admiration should be seen in the context of their using him as a foil for their own great leaders, especially Richard the Lionheart. It was a common trope in Medieval Europe to set up a great enemy as a chastisement from God for wicked Christian leaders. Admiring Saladin was perhaps also a way for the Franks to portray themselves as having the superior religion because they could see quality in an enemy and to show that chivalry was a universal code in all upper classes through the world.

This does not mean that any of the Christians who admired Saladin as a good villain and a model of chivalry thought that his religion was better than theirs. In fact, after Britain took Jerusalem from the Ottoman Empire, rumors of leaders like British General Allenby and French General Henri Gouraud proclaiming their final victory in the Crusades over Saladin became popular. These reflected both Arab resentment of European colonialism and European feelings of superiority over the Middle East.

Still, for the most part the European view of Saladin was positive. Dante portrayed him as a virtuous pagan in *The Divine Comedy*, as did the *chansons*. Sir Walter Scott cast him as a mysterious helper for the Scottish hero knight of his novel, *The Talisman* (1825). Scott used his characterization of Saladin's civilized nature as a way to accentuate the vices of his evil Templar villains.

As pan-Arab nationalism arose in the wake of the failure of the Ottoman Empire and the rise of European colonialism in the Middle East, Muslims took this romanticized view of Saladin to heart. Anti-Crusades ideology has fueled much anti-Western anger in the past century, culminating in Osama bin Laden's illogical call to jihad, and Saladin became the symbol and hero for those who sought to fight the West, just as Saladin had done so successfully so long ago.

Saladin has been especially honored in Egypt, where he has been erroneously hailed as a homegrown hero ever since Gamal Abdel Nasser took Saladin's eagle standard as the symbol for Nasserism. He is also extremely popular in Iraq, where he was born. Despite being secular rulers, Egyptian strong man Nasser (1918-1970) and Iraqi dictator Saddam Hussein (1937-2006) both played up their associations with Saladin to increase their popularity (Hussein, like Saladin, was born in Tikrit). Hussein also favored another conqueror of Jerusalem as his historical idol: the biblical Nebuchadnezzar. As with most historical comparisons, those who have taken Saladin as their historical role model have said more about themselves than about Saladin.

Today, Saladin is an extremely popular idol in the Middle East, one that obscures the true man and shrewd general behind the myth. Saladin's personality was a complex one, but many have tried to simplify it for good or ill. To his biographers and to many of his Christian rivals, he was the soul of chivalry and also in a more condescending sense a medieval version of the "Noble Savage" in European literature. This version of Saladin appeared, with no trace of irony, in works as diverse as William of Tyre, Jan Lievens' fanciful 17th century portrait of a dark-skinned African Saladin holding a pious Guy de Lusignan captive in golden chains after Hattin, Sir Walter Scott's *The Talisman*, and the recent film *Kingdom of Heaven* (2005). In these, he is portrayed as a mild-mannered pacifist, even a healer, reluctantly turning to war in the face of obstinate and savage Christian foes.

Lievens' portrait of Saladin and Guy

The religion of the source is important in this view. In the Christian view, Saladin is intended to show up Christian hypocrites who kill in the name of their religion, violating their own beliefs (*If a pagan can act like this, Christian knights should be ashamed to sink so much lower,* goes the lesson), but he is not intended to show that Islam is superior to Christianity. He is portrayed as an embarrassing example, or a weapon of God, but not really a human hero to be emulated.

The opposite is the case in the Islamic world, where Saladin is raised to truly mythic heights. Many of the less comfortable aspects of his background and life have been completely ignored, including the important facts that he was not an Arab, that he conquered Egypt and destroyed her independence, that he was a rebellious vassal, that some of the things attributed to him were the accomplishments of others who may even have been his enemies, and that he spent as much of his career fighting other Muslims as he did fighting Christians. Like everyone else who is turned into a symbol after death, the inconvenient stuff is simply altered or ignored for the sake of the narrative.

The negative sources are fewer, but vociferous. In them, Saladin is a savage Kurd, a usurper, even a plotter and a poisoner who was vicious to his enemies and even a precursor to the Antichrist. In some sources, such as Ibn al-Athir (who wrote after Saladin's death and was not entirely contemporary), Saladin is portrayed as weak and irreligious, gaining power mainly through nepotism.

This portrayal is obviously not fully accurate, either, but it must be considered. Saladin was educated and cultured in many ways. There is considerable evidence that he respected Islamic learning and certain aspects of Arab culture, that he showed mercy when he did not have to and diplomacy even with his enemies. And he did end his life humbly. But he also has a darker side.

He did not rise to power through his education or his culture. He rose through the connections of his family, and through force and guile, which were common tools of his time though they may appear distasteful today. Several notable and brutal examples exist to show that Saladin's mercy could be arbitrary and affected by his personal feelings. There were times when he chose to dehumanize entire groups of people through his rhetoric, even civilians, which he then massacred or enslaved if they angered him. Contrary to some of the mythmaking, his actions show high ambition, and he was frequently the aggressor on his campaigns. These are all things that were indicative of his contemporaries, both Muslim and Christian, as well, and Saladin does not appear to have been as brutal as a Zengi or a Reynaud de Chatillon. But he was nonetheless far more bloody than the myth. This is an important consideration when placing him in the context of his times. He was often a great hero, but he could also be a great villain, and not all of his victims deserved their fates.

One thing that does shine through in most sources is that he was a great general and a well-respected leader. His enemies respected his military prowess and his own army loved him. And though he died before completing his goal of destroying the Crusader states in Palestine, and though it would take another century before his descendants accomplished this, he did succeed in breaking the backs of the Crusader States and uniting, however briefly, Egypt with Syria. These things were not small accomplishments. After Saladin, the Crusaders attempted to continue on, and did for quite some time, but a combination of unfortunate events, waning interest in Europe, and the effectiveness of Saladin's campaigns ultimately doomed Christian Palestine. It is, in large part, Saladin who is responsible for Islam dominating the Middle East today.

It is still difficult at this point to discern his true motivations under the layers of diplomacy, political expediency and pious propaganda, especially at critical moments of his career, such as his sudden rise in Egypt in the wake of his uncle's death. But Saladin was no more paradoxical than any other great ruler in history, and he is generally considered, both by his contemporaries and by subsequent writers, to be one of the most remarkable figures of his age. His dream was to conquer all of the Levant and bring it back, both under Muslim rule and under a strong Muslim ruler. For him, strong Muslim rule meant a single ruler. He came very close to succeeding, and he laid the foundations for his descendants to complete his dream, albeit at a cost none of them could foresee.

Saladin's entire career was affected by the nature of medieval Islamic politics, where there was little administrative continuity between one secular ruler and the next, even within a hereditary dynasty. Unlike Christian Europe, the Qur'an laid out strict rules on how individuals and groups in the *ummah* (the community of Islam) should treat each other, but there was no secular, or even larger religious, power to enforce this. Thus, there was no legal mechanism to deter a Muslim ruler from becoming a tyrant. This also meant that a ruler could institute very quick and decisive reforms, but these reforms were dependent on his (or her, since a few female Muslim rulers did exist) force of personality. They could easily be reversed or allowed to fade by a weak or hostile successor.

Saladin lived in a militarized culture of Turkish mercenaries, where the strongest rulers fought on the field of battle and jockeyed for position with their rivals as much as they allied with them. Minors or religious leaders like the caliphs (descendants of the Prophet Muhammad) were used as puppets. A strong ruler could easily eliminate the previous government of his predecessor and institute his own. In Saladin's culture, a king ruled by decree.

It is perhaps the greatest paradox of Saladin's life and career that he excelled at exploiting this idiosyncrasy of Islamic politics, yet the same aspect ultimately destroyed his own legacy in the Middle East within a century of his death. Amazingly enough, it would be his foremost adversaries that helped keep his name and legacy alive.

Bibliography

Barber, Malcolm. *The Crusader States*. Yale University Press, 2012.

Eddé, Anne-Marie. *Saladin*. Belknap Press of Harvard University Press, 2011.

Hindley, Geoffrey. *Saladin: Hero of Islam*. Pen and Sword, 2010.

Kedar, B.Z. *The Horns of Hattin*. Variorum, 1992.

Maalouf, Amin. *The Crusades through Arab Eyes*. Schocken Books, 1984.

Nicolle, David. Saladin: *The Background, Strategies, Tactics and Battlefield Experiences of the Greatest Commanders of History.* Osprey Publishing, 2011.

Online Resources

Ed-Din, Beha. *The Life of Saladin*. Palestine Pilgrims' Society, 1897.
http://archive.org/details/libraryofpalesti13paleuoft

Gibb, Sir Hamilton. *The Life of Saladin: From the Works of Imad ad-Din and Baha ad-Din*. Clarendon Press, 1973. http://www.ghazali.org/books/gibb-73.pdf

Lawson, Rich. *Richard and Saladin: Warriors of the Crusade*. (Retrieved 8/31/2012) http://www.shadowedrealm.com/articles/exclusive/richard_saladin_warriors_third_crusade

Lev, Yaacov. *Saladin in Egypt*. Brill, 1999.
http://books.google.com/books/about/Saladin_in_Egypt.html?id=v22DckibeIUC

Lyons, M.C. and Jackson, D.E.P. *Saladin: The Politics of the Holy War*. Cambridge University Press, 1982.
http://books.google.com/books?id=hGR5M0druJIC&printsec=frontcover#v=onepage&q&f=false